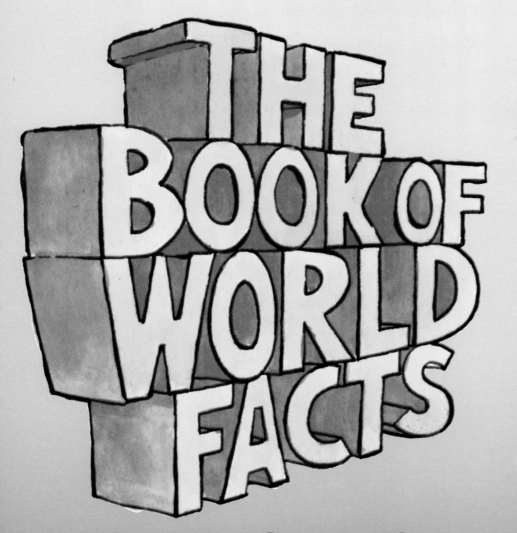

THE BOOK OF WORLD FACTS

Anita Ganeri

Contents

CAMBRIDGE
UNIVERSITY PRESS

UCL
Institute of Education

T0384560

Our Amazing World

The world is an amazing place. It has countries and cities. It has long rivers, high mountains and dry deserts.

Have you ever wondered which country is the biggest? Which lake is saltier than the sea? Which is the coldest place in the world?

This book is full of amazing facts about the world we live in.

Cities

Cities are like very big towns. They have homes, offices, shops and parks.

Millions of people live in cities. Many people travel to cities to go to work.

City records
Biggest city: Tokyo, Japan
Smallest city: Hum, Croatia

The most important city in a country is called the capital city. Tokyo is the capital city of Japan. It has a **population** of nearly 40 million. Hum has a population of less than 25.

Look how busy it is!

Tokyo

Countries

Russia is the biggest country in the world. If someone wanted to drive from one side of Russia to another, it would take two weeks!

Country records
Biggest country: Russia
Most people: China

China

China has more people living there than any other country.
More than **one billion** people live in China.

Deserts

A desert is a place that does not get much rain. Some deserts are hot during the day, some are cold. All deserts are very cold at night. Some deserts are sandy. Some deserts are rocky.

rocky desert

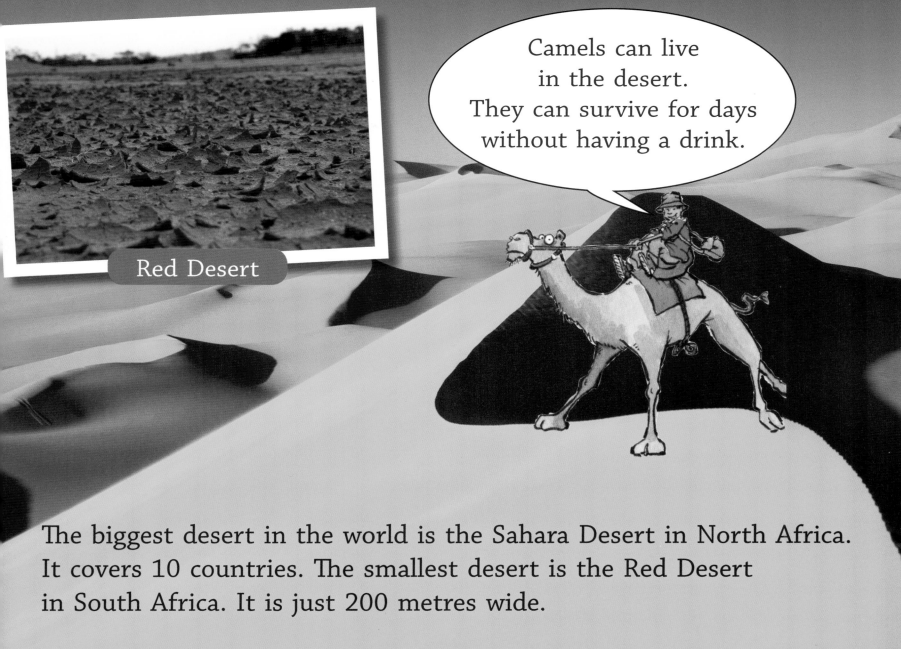

Red Desert

Camels can live in the desert. They can survive for days without having a drink.

The biggest desert in the world is the Sahara Desert in North Africa. It covers 10 countries. The smallest desert is the Red Desert in South Africa. It is just 200 metres wide.

Lakes

A lake is a patch of water in a dip in the ground. Some lakes are filled with **fresh water**. Some are filled with salty water.

Moscow

Russia

Lake Baikal

Caspian
Sea

Lake facts
Biggest lake: Caspian Sea, Western Asia
Deepest lake: Lake Baikal, Russia

This lake is much saltier than the sea. It is called the Dead Sea. It is so salty that you cannot sink in it.

Mountains

A mountain is an area of land that is high up. Mount Everest is the highest mountain in the world.

It is cold and windy on a high mountain.

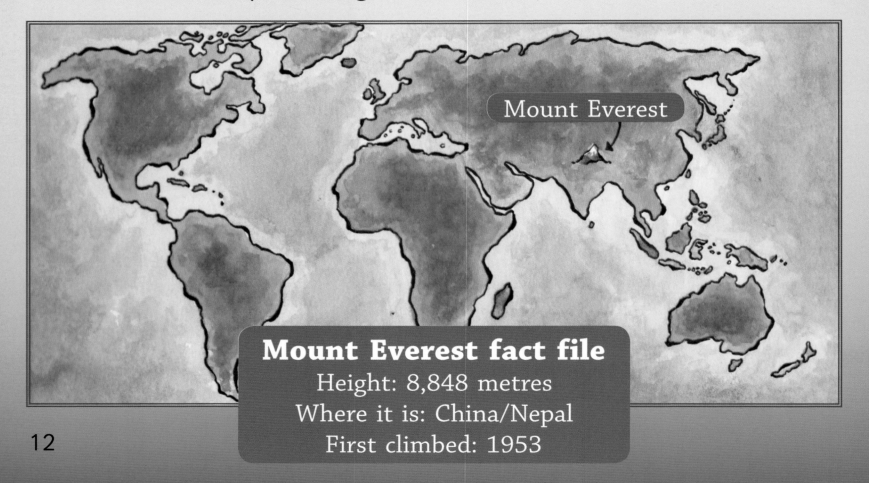

Mount Everest

Mount Everest fact file
Height: 8,848 metres
Where it is: China/Nepal
First climbed: 1953

Yaks need thick, woolly coats to keep them warm.

Mount Everest is as tall as as 900 houses stacked one on top of the other.

Oceans

An ocean is a very big area of sea.

The biggest ocean is called the Pacific Ocean.
It reaches halfway around the world.
The water in an ocean is salty.

The five oceans
Pacific
Atlantic
Indian
Southern
Arctic

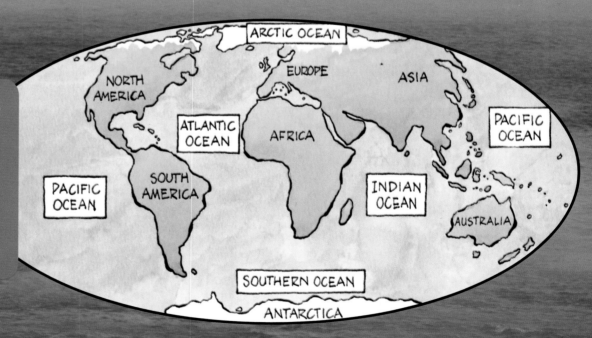

Some deep-sea animals make their own light.

Some places in the ocean are warm and some are cold.
Deep in the ocean, the water is dark and freezing cold.

Poles

The poles are
the places at the top
and bottom
of the world.
The North Pole, also
called the Arctic, is at
the top of the world.
The South Pole,
also called Antarctica,
is at the bottom.
The Poles are
the coldest places
in the world.

Antarctica

scientist

It is too cold to live in Antarctica all of the time.
But some **scientists** go there to work.
They study the weather, the ice and the **wildlife**.

Rainforests

Rainforests grow around the middle of the Earth, where it is always hot. It rains almost every day.

Many different kinds of animal live in the rainforest.

The biggest rainforest is the Amazon.
It grows across nine countries in South America.

COCOA TREE

BANANA TREE

BRAZIL NUTS

Brazil nuts, bananas and chocolate all come from plants that grow in the rainforest.

Rivers

A river is made up of fresh water. It flows across the land. Many rivers start high up in the mountains. Most rivers flow into the sea.

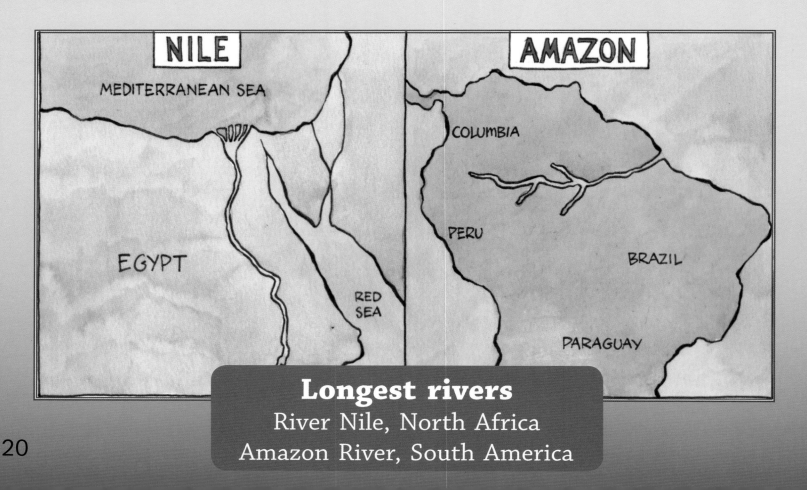

Longest rivers
River Nile, North Africa
Amazon River, South America

The River Nile runs through nine countries and ends in Egypt in the Mediterranean Sea. It is home to many animals and birds.

Amazon River

Most rivers run from north to south, but the Nile runs from south to north.

21

Glossary

one billion   a thousand million

fresh water   water that is not salty

population   all the people living in a place

scientists   people who use science to learn things about the world

wildlife   plants and animals

yaks   long-haired cow-like animals

Index

The Book of World Facts Anita Ganeri

Teaching notes written by Sue Bodman and Glen Franklin

Using this book

Developing reading comprehension

This compendium brings together interesting geographical facts, arranged thematically, that will be of interest to children wherever they live. A mix of photographs, illustrations, maps and charts serve to provide information. This book is a good starting point for children to carry out further in-depth study into areas of interest.

Grammar and sentence structure

- Longer, more complex sentences incorporate adjectives and adverbial phrases.
- Captions and labels are punctuated correctly according to purpose.

Word meaning and spelling

- Spelling of comparative and superlative adjectives ('*saltier*', '*highest*'), exploring changes to the root words (for example, doubling the consonant when writing '*biggest*').
- Reading of novel or unfamiliar, multi-syllabic words ('*population*'; '*Antarctica*') and ensuring these are understood through use of the context and the glossary.

Curriculum links

Geography – Use the sections of the book to introduce more in-depth study of particular areas of interest, such as work on rainforests.

Literacy – The short sections detailing each World Fact could become the basis for report writing, comparing and contrasting the layout, grammar and style of other reports on the same subject.

Learning outcomes

Children can:

- recognise how specific language is used to present information in non-fiction texts
- take note of punctuation, using it to keep track of longer sentences and noting impact

- attempt unfamiliar words, including those not completely decodable, monitoring that their meaning is understood.

A guided reading lesson

Book Introduction

Note: how you use this book in guided reading will depend on the children's own experiences and on your teaching purpose in selecting it for your lesson. A good starting point for working with this book would be to begin with a region that is familiar to the children. These teacher notes will assume that the children live in a city.

Orientation

Give each child a copy of the book. Ask them to read the title and the blurb. Look through the book quickly together, ascertaining that this is an information book, and noting some of the key features of non-fiction texts, as well as the less-familiar features such as the inclusion of cartoon illustrations. Remind the children of the purpose of reading for information, and that non-fiction books are generally not read from beginning to end.

Turn to the contents page and skim the contents. Say: *There are lots of interesting things to find out about our world. Today we are going to look at people who live in a city like us. But first, let's look at the introduction.*

Preparation

Pages 2 and 3: Read the heading '*Our Amazing World*'. Ask the children to read pages 2 and 3 quietly and then to tell you some of the amazing things they might read about in this book. Explain that today you will be looking at the section about cities.

Pages 4 and 5: Say: *We live in a city, don't we? What do we know about living in a city? How is it different from living in the countryside/by the sea/in the mountains?* Draw out the children's prior knowledge and experience. Then ask them to read the pages with their partner.

After reading, ask if there were any interesting things about cities that the author has not included.